LET'S-READ-AND-FIND-OUT SCIENCE®

STAGE 2

REVISED EDITION

Where Does the Garbage Go?

by Paul Showers

illustrated by Randy Chewning

HarperCollins*Publishers*

Special thanks to Robin Woods of the United States Environmental Protection Agency and William Rathje, founder of the Garbage Project at the University of Arizona, for their expert advice and information.

The illustrations in this book were prepared with Winsor and Newton Brilliant Watercolours and a .35 pen on two-ply Strathmore 500 Bristol paper.

The *Let's-Read-and-Find-Out Science* book series was originated by Dr. Franklyn M. Branley, Astronomer Emeritus and former Chairman of the American Museum–Hayden Planetarium, and was formerly co-edited by him and Dr. Roma Gans, Professor Emeritus of Childhood Education, Teachers College, Columbia University. Text and illustrations for each of the books in the series are checked for accuracy by an expert in the relevant field. For a complete catalog of Let's-Read-and-Find-Out Science books, write to HarperCollins Children's Books, 10 East 53rd Street, New York, NY 10022.

Let's-Read-and-Find-Out Science is a registered trademark of HarperCollins Publishers.

Library of Congress Cataloging-in-Publication Data
Showers, Paul.
    Where does the garbage go? / by Paul Showers ; illustrated by Randy Chewning. — Rev. ed.
        p.   cm. — (Let's-read-and-find-out science. Stage 2)
    Summary: Explains how people create too much waste and how waste is now recycled and put into landfills.
    ISBN 0-06-021054-0. — ISBN 0-06-021057-5 (lib. bdg.). — ISBN 0-06-445114-3 (pbk.)
    1. Refuse and refuse disposal—Juvenile literature.   [1. Refuse and refuse disposal.   2. Recycling (Waste)]
I. Chewning, Randy, ill.   II. Title.   III. Series.
TD792.S48   1994   91-46115
628.4'4—dc20   CIP
                                                                                         AC

1   2   3   4   5   6   7   8   9   10
❖
Revised Edition

Where Does the Garbage Go?

In our school we are learning about garbage.

Last week our teacher told us about the way things used to be.

Garbage.
Where does it come from?
Where does it go?

She said there was a time when people who wanted to get rid of something just threw it into the garbage can. They threw in garbage like orange peels, chicken bones, the food they didn't eat. They threw in trash, too—empty bottles, tin cans, cardboard boxes, old newspapers.

When you put garbage

and trash together,

you call it waste.

Once a week the waste was collected in trucks and taken out to the dump.

In the dump there were piles of garbage everywhere and all kinds of trash—old tires, broken bottles, tin cans, old newspapers, broken chairs and sofas. In summer the garbage rotted and made a terrible stink. Rats came to eat it. Millions of flies buzzed around. The dump was a great big mess.

Today some towns still have dumps where they leave their garbage and trash.

At one time New York City used the ocean for its dump. It loaded its waste on flat boats called barges. Tugboats pulled the barges out to sea, and the waste was dumped overboard. Most of the trash sank, but some of it floated.

ugh!

Often it floated right back to the beaches where people were swimming. *Ugh! Yeccch!*

New York City doesn't throw its waste in the ocean anymore. It has a special kind of dump called a landfill. Other cities have landfills, too. Our town has one, and our class went out and looked at it.

A landfill is a busy place.

Not a great place for a picnic!

Phew! It smells.

Trucks bring loads of waste from the city and dump it in big piles.

Bulldozers with scrapers spread out the waste.

Compactors with spikes on their wheels move back and forth over it. The waste is all mashed and piled.

13

After that, trucks bring loads of soil. The bulldozers and compactors spread the soil over the waste. The soil covers up everything. It keeps out the rats and flies.

Then the landfill is ready for more waste. Then comes more soil to cover it up—then more waste and more soil, layer after layer. A landfill keeps piling up. It gets to be a little mountain.

The layers of a landfill

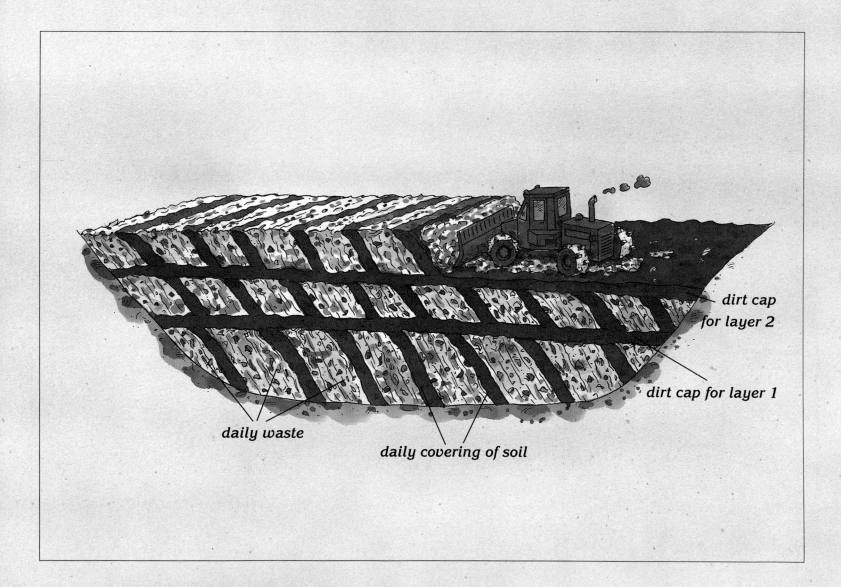

daily waste

daily covering of soil

dirt cap
for layer 2

dirt cap for layer 1

When the last layer of soil is spread on top of a landfill, grass and trees are planted on it. The landfill becomes a park or a playground.

Then the city has to start a new landfill. Waste never stops piling up.

What is in our landfills?

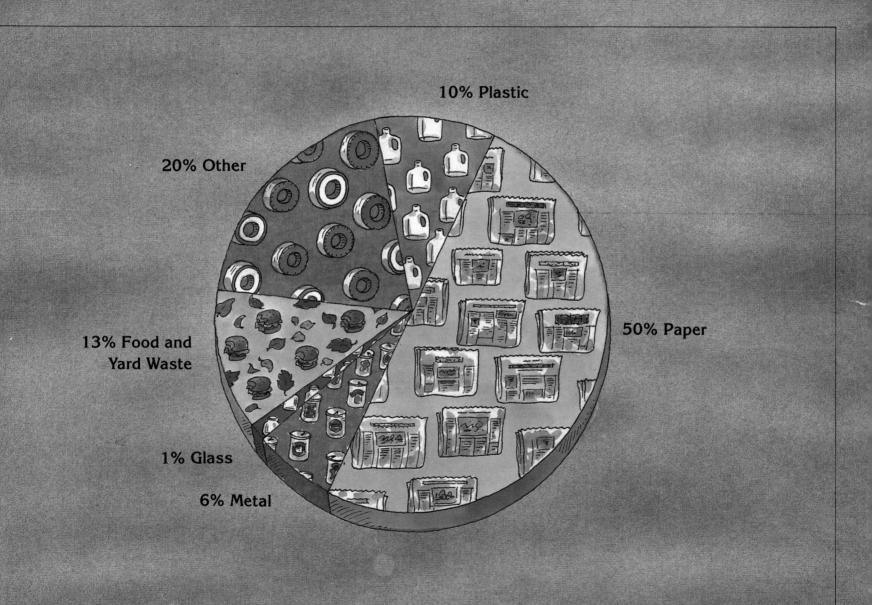

10% Plastic

20% Other

50% Paper

13% Food and
Yard Waste

1% Glass

6% Metal

Some cities try to get rid of their waste by burning it. They build big furnaces called incinerators and burn garbage and trash in them. The heat is used to warm stores and offices. It is also used to make electricity.

How an incinerator works

trucks bring garbage

furnace burns garbage in about 30 minutes

garbage is fed to a furnace

But incinerators don't really get rid of everything. They simply turn the waste into ashes, and the ashes have to go to a landfill. Sometimes those ashes are toxic or harmful. And sometimes the smoke from the incinerator pollutes the air with harmful gases.

cleaned gases are released

gases from the burning garbage must be carefully cleaned and filtered

Today cities are having a hard time finding places for new landfills. Waste keeps piling up. People keep throwing things away. They throw away too many things. Some of the things they throw away could be used over again.

Each person in the U.S. creates about four pounds of trash every day.

Many cities are now trying something that is new for them. It is called recycling. Recycling means making trash into something new instead of throwing it away.

Almost half of the trash we throw away could be recycled. Look for this symbol on glass, metal, and plastic containers that can be recycled.

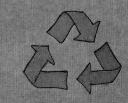

Our city is recycling. We still put garbage in the garbage can—orange peels, chicken bones, the food we don't eat. But we keep empty glass bottles in a separate box. Aluminum cans and foil are kept separate, too. When we put the cans and bottles at the curb, we pile old newspapers beside them. We flatten our cardboard boxes and pile them next to the newspapers.

When the garbage truck comes, it picks up only the garbage and takes it out to the landfill. Other trucks come for the bottles and cans and newspapers. Those things don't go to the landfill anymore. Our city sells them to factories and mills for recycling.

Paper mills chop up old newspapers and turn them into new paper.

paper is shredded into pulp

pulp is washed and bleached

water is drained from pulp

paper is dried and rolled

Aluminum factories take aluminum cans and foil and melt them to make new cans and rolls of foil.

cans are chopped

decoater takes off paint from metal scraps with hot air (900° F)

melted aluminum is poured into molds

scraps are melted in furnace (1220° F)

Glass bottles are ground up and melted to make new glass bottles and jars.

other glass bottles are crushed

glass is melted in a furnace

some bottles are sterilized and reused

blown-in air cools glass

gobs of molten glass are poured into molds

Even plastic can be recycled. Plastic factories chop it up and turn it into things like flowerpots and park benches.

plastic is chopped
into bits

bits are washed
and dried

plastic is melted and
poured into a mold

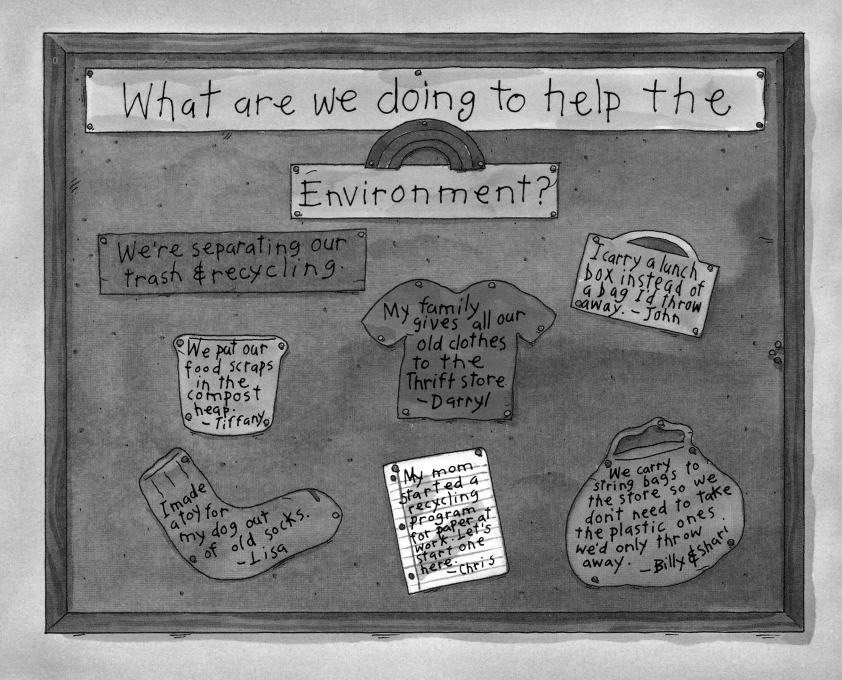

Our teacher says recycling is a good start, but we must do more. We must stop making so much waste. We must stop throwing so many things away. We need to find ways to use things over and over again.

Need a bag kids?

10.07

Whole Wheat Bread

That's what we have done at home. We used to bring our groceries home in paper and plastic bags. When we emptied the bags, we threw them in the garbage can. When we did that, we were just making more waste to pile up in the landfill.

We have stopped doing that. Now we use string bags. They hang on the kitchen doorknob. When we go to the supermarket, we take our string bags and put our groceries in them.

31

We never throw away our string bags. They are strong and hold a lot of groceries. We use them over and over again.